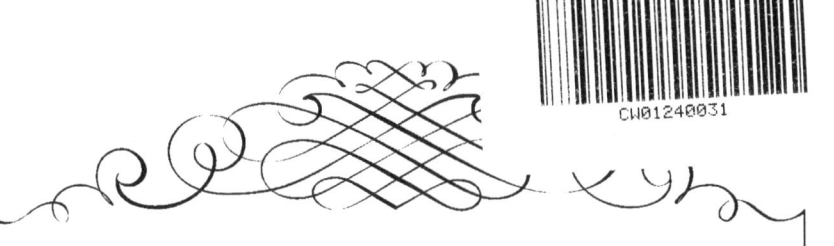

797,885 Books
are available to read at

Forgotten Books

www.ForgottenBooks.com

Forgotten Books' App
Available for mobile, tablet & eReader

ISBN 978-1-332-91144-8
PIBN 10436887

This book is a reproduction of an important historical work. Forgotten Books uses state-of-the-art technology to digitally reconstruct the work, preserving the original format whilst repairing imperfections present in the aged copy. In rare cases, an imperfection in the original, such as a blemish or missing page, may be replicated in our edition. We do, however, repair the vast majority of imperfections successfully; any imperfections that remain are intentionally left to preserve the state of such historical works.

Forgotten Books is a registered trademark of FB &c Ltd.
Copyright © 2017 FB &c Ltd.
FB &c Ltd, Dalton House, 60 Windsor Avenue, London, SW19 2RR.
Company number 08720141. Registered in England and Wales.

For support please visit www.forgottenbooks.com

1 MONTH OF FREE READING

at

www.ForgottenBooks.com

By purchasing this book you are eligible for one month membership to ForgottenBooks.com, giving you unlimited access to our entire collection of over 700,000 titles via our web site and mobile apps.

To claim your free month visit:
www.forgottenbooks.com/free436887

* Offer is valid for 45 days from date of purchase. Terms and conditions apply.

English
Français
Deutsche
Italiano
Español
Português

www.forgottenbooks.com

Mythology Photography **Fiction** Fishing Christianity **Art** Cooking Essays Buddhism Freemasonry Medicine **Biology** Music **Ancient Egypt** Evolution Carpentry Physics Dance Geology **Mathematics** Fitness Shakespeare **Folklore** Yoga Marketing **Confidence** Immortality Biographies Poetry **Psychology** Witchcraft Electronics Chemistry History **Law** Accounting **Philosophy** Anthropology Alchemy Drama Quantum Mechanics Atheism Sexual Health **Ancient History Entrepreneurship** Languages Sport Paleontology Needlework Islam **Metaphysics** Investment Archaeology Parenting Statistics Criminology **Motivational**

GREAT TRIUMPH

STEINWAY & SONS
MANUFACTURERS OF
GRAND, SQUARE AND UPRIGHT
PIANO FORTE
NEW YORK.

This Firm commenced manufacturing Pianos in the year
their capacity was then less than one instrument per week, they
turn out from forty to fifty per week, including from five to six (
CERT GRANDS. They employ the most skillful workmen
number at least one-third of all employed in that business in
York city), and all the latest improved machinery and every fac
enabling them to manufacture the best Piano Fortes in the worl

THEIR MANUFACTORY

occupies the entire block on Fourth Avenue, from Fifty-Sec
Fifty-Third streets, and is one of the largest and best arranged
world. The main building is five stories high, and covers fo
city lots; twelve other lots being used for the purpose of sea
lumber, of which there is a stock of about 2,000,000 feet alwa
hand. Four Drying Houses, each heated by 2000 feet of ste
are constantly used in the process of drying the lumber.

STEINWAY & SONS,

From a small beginning but a few years since, is now the most extensive establishment in the United States, or in Europe. Their extensive Warerooms were found inadequate to their immense trade, to supply which they have erected a splendid white marble building in a central and pleasant part of the city,

Nos. 71 and 73 East Fourteenth Street,

Between Union Square and the Academy of Music,

Where, with their increased facilities, they take great pleasure in exhibiting to the public their *Unrivalled Instruments.*

THE STEINWAY PIANO

is now recommended and used almost exclusively by the principal Pianists, including Mr. S. B. MILLS, the great artist and teacher, WILLIAM MASON, ROBERT HELLER, J. N. PATTISON, and others of distinction in this country; also HANS V. BULOW, ALFRED JAELL and GUSTAV SATTER, and many others of equal celebrity in Europe.

The history of the world has never recorded such a growth and splendid triumph in business; and the only way to account for it is, that the firm is composed of practical Piano Forte makers (father and sons), who invent all their own improvements, under whose personal supervision every part of the instrument is manufactured, and who so far from relaxing their efforts to turn out perfect instruments, even increase their care and exertions with the immense increase of their business.

STEINWAY & SONS

Would respectfully call the attention of the public to their Improved

GRAND, SQUARE AND UPRIGHT

PIANOS

(with full iron frame) which for volume of tone, elasticity of touch, and beauty of finish, in short everything that renders a Piano perfect, are unsurpassed. By an ingenious arrangement of their scales they succeed in combining the durability and sweet singing tone of the Iron Frame Piano with the full rich sound of the Wooden Frame, a result not attained by any of the numerous makers who have tried to imitate and copy their scales and patterns, in proof of which they refer with pleasure to a few of the many testimonials in their possession from distinguished citizens and well known musical celebreties:

BROOKLYN, January 26, 1861.

MESSRS. STEINWAY:

I regard him as a benefactor who builds a good piano, and I am your beneficiary on that account. Having had one of your instruments for several years I can bear witness to its admirable qualities in every respect. I am more than satisfied, and if I had to buy another, I should certainly go to your rooms again. It is a pleasure to praise your work.

HENRY WARD BEECHER.

For more extended Notices and Testimonials, see pages 14, 15 and 16.

PART I.

FULL CHORUS TO LIBERTY—By all the Characters.
Air—"*Grand March in Norma.*"

CHORUS.

Raise the song, raise the song,
  Raise with grateful hearts the thankful song of praise,
All the gifts of earth, here, by right of birth
  Springing, blooming, gushing, flowing, crown the cup.
Then impart thou the blessing sent by heaven,
  With gentle hand the drooping soul sustaining;
Raise thy voice, till to every man shall equal rights be given,
  Till in thy universal reign the world be blest.

SEMI-CHORUS.

All hail to thee, O Liberty,
  With every bliss on earth abounding,
All good the patriot heart desires
  Is here thy path surrounding.

LIBERTY.

Well done, all my children! your steps and your voices
  Make glad all the hearts that love freedom and truth!
Beneath your glad smiles, all the wide world rejoices,
  And the old turn again to the glory of youth.

Still shine like a star to the souls that lie mourning,
  And pierce with your brightness Oppression's dark night
In peace or in war—still with loathing and scorning,
  Dash off every charm that would fetter your might.

I have looked on the land where the tyrant was ruling,
  His foot on the necks of the honest and true;
Heaven save *you*, my children, from clashing and falling!
  Let the hand of Oppression ne'er rest upon *you!*

Wide—wide o'er the empires that crumble to ruin,
  My kingdom shall flourish, from sea unto sea,
And every dark land, all its evils undoing,
  Shall thenceforth be bright with the light of the free!

SONG OF TRUTH AND JUSTICE—With Chorus.
Air—"*Yankee Doodle.*"

Song—We stand together hand in hand,
  As we have stood for ages,
To battle for the right, while might
  Against us vainly rages.

Chorus of States—Let the mighty despots rage,
    We will serve them never;
    Truth and Justice lead the way
    And be our guide forever.

Song—We stand beside our royal Queen
    As fearless and undaunted
    As when upon New England's rock
    By her our feet were planted.

Chorus of States—Truth and Justice and our Queen
    Shall be conquered never;
    We will follow where they lead
    And be victorious ever.

RESPONSE OF STATES IN THE ORDER OF THEIR ADMISSION INTO THE UNION.

DELAWARE.

Delaware, eldest and least of thy band,
  Pledges her all as she owns thy command;
And craves if thou would'st her devotion requite,
  To watch if she shrinks from the van of the fight.

PENNSYLVANIA.

From Independence Hall again
  Shall ring out Freedom's note;
And o'er the land of William Penn
  What tyrant flag dare float?

NEW JERSEY.

New Jersey tells of Trenton,
  And of Monmouth brave and true.
No prouder name can any bear
  Than that of Jersey blue!

GEORGIA.

Pulaski lies within my breast:
  If aliens so for thee could die,
What should thy offspring shrink to dare,
  In thy great cause, O, Liberty.

CONNECTICUT.

The Charter Oak has fallen low;
  Not so the charter of our rights;
Try how the Wooden-Nutmeg State
  For Law, for Truth and Freedom fights!

MASSACHUSETTS.

Old Massachusetts proudly points
  To Plymouth Rock, her glory still,
And gives the world the deathless names
  Of Lexington and Bunker Hill.

MARYLAND.
As rolls my broad Potomac wave
  Majestic to the Sea,
So Maryland would see thy cause
  Advance — O, Liberty!

SOUTH CAROLINA.
The old South State had Marion
  And Sumter in the past;
Try if she has not men *as* true,
  When *rings* the bugle blast!

NEW HAMPSHIRE.
From where my granite mountains rise,
  One, bright with Washington's great name,
Shall ever float on loftiest peak —
  Thy cherished flag of starry flame.

SONG AND CHORUS.
AIR—"*Viva L'America.*"

Noble Republic! happiest of lands!
Foremost of nations, Columbia stands;
Freedom's proud banner floats in the skies,
Where shouts of liberty daily arise.
"United we stand, divided we fall,"
Union for ever, freedom to all.
Throughout the world our motto shall be,
Viva L'America, Home of the free!

CHORUS.
Throughout the world our motto shall be,
Viva L'America, Home of the free!

Should ever traitor rise in the land,
Cursed be his homestead, wither'd his hand;
Shame be his memory, scorn be his lot —
Exhile his heritage, his name a blot!
"United we stand, divided we fall,"
Granting a home and freedom to all.
Throughout the world our motto shall be,
Viva L'America, Home of the free!

CHORUS.
Throughout the world our motto shall be,
Viva L'America, Home of the free!

VIRGINIA.
Virginia in her glorious past
  Reared many a noble son;
And yet her crowning boast at last,
  She points to *Washington.*

NEW YORK.

On me the broad Atlantic wave with Erie's waters meet,
And proud Niagara's thundering tide comes down to wash my feet.
The forked lightning heeds my will, I ride in power the wave;
Prouder than all, men cannot call my meanest subject slave.

NORTH CAROLINA.

The pines are thick upon my hills,
 My swamps are dark and low;
The one will scourge, the other drown,
 Whoever comes thy foe.

RHODE ISLAND.

Let little Rhody lift her voice!
 Small packages for goods of price!
And when the country calls—look out!
 That little hand *grips* like a vice!

VERMONT.

Vermont's green mountains kiss the sun;
 Their emerald hue new grace imparts;
And yet not greener is their sod
 Than love for thee within our hearts.

KENTUCKY.

My fields and valleys blossom like the rose,
 Since they unrolled before the pioneer
Who brought me brawny arms and dauntless hearts,
 And taught me first thy banner to revere.

TENNESSEE.

Virginia's blue peaks clasp my own,
 The Mississippi bathes my feet;
And both shall bear thy star-gemmed flag
 That binds the States in concord sweet.

OHIO.

I'll strip my vineyards of their purplest yield
 To pledge the deathless bond that blends our fate;
Call when thou wilt—thy faintest word or look
 Shall rouse the leal and fearless Buckeye State.

LOUISIANA, MISSISSIPPI, ALABAMA AND TEXAS.

The Gulf States, hand in hand,
Will march at thy command,
Thy temples wreath with bays,
Thy standard higher raise.

FULL CHORUS.
AIR—"*America.*"

My country, 'tis of thee
Sweet land of liberty,
Of thee I sing;
Land where my fathers died;
Land of the pilgrims' pride;
From every mountain side
Let Freedom ring.

Our Fathers' God! to thee,
Author of Liberty,
To thee we sing;
Long may our land be bright
With Freedom's holy light,
Protect us by thy might,
Great God our King.

INDIANA.

As fled the red skins from the fight,
Where fierce Tecumseh bravely fell;
So will my gallant Hoosier boys
Crush all who 'gainst thy sway rebel.

ILLINOIS.

My prairies rich, my teeming soil,
My lakes that marry with the sea,
Shall bear no flag whate'er betide,
Save thine—blest banner of the free.

MAINE.

From where her pine trees echo back
The moan from wild Atlantic's sea—
Through cold and storm, with unchill'd heart,
Maine comes to thee, O, Liberty!

MISSOURI.

My plains are rich and fertile, my rivers broad and fine,
I've iron for thy armor and for thy banquets, wine;
I've grain to feed thy armies, I've sons who'll heed thy call,
If you but whisper battle, they'll win the fight or fall.

ARKANSAS.

I am a little rough down-easters say;
I 'spose 'tis so; but be that as it may,
Whoever dare assert your word aint law,
Must dodge the toothpick of old Arkansas.

MICHIGAN.

My necklace blue of noble lakes
Shall bear thy fleets with jealous care;
My sons shall fill thy valiant ranks,
And in the van thy colors bear.

FLORIDA.

Of Ponce de Leon's fount of youth,
By poets sweetly sung,
Thy lips have drank, and evermore,
Thou'rt deathless, fair and young.

CALIFORNIA.

Hark! heard ye not the chink of gold?
Thy coffers shall have every bar,
And sturdy arms to bear thy flag
When peril threatens stripe or star.

SONG AND CHORUS—The Flag of the Free.

    Nobly our flag flutters o'er us to-day,
      Emblem of peace, Pledge of Liberty's sway,
    Its foes shall tremble and shrink in dismay,
      If e'er insulted it be!
    Our "stripes and stars," lov'd and honor'd by all,
    Shall float forever where freedom may call,
    It still shall be the flag of the free,
      Emblem of sweet Liberty.
CHORUS.—Here we will gather its cause to defend,
      Let patriots rally and wise counsels lend,
      It still shall be the flag of the free—
      Emblem of sweet Liberty.

    With it in beauty no flag can compare,
    All nations honor our banner so fair,
    If to insult it, a traitor should dare,
      Crush'd to the earth let him be!
    "Freedom and Progress," our watchword to-day,
    When duty calls us who dares disobey?
    Honor to thee, thou flag of the free,
      Emblem of sweet Liberty.
  CHORUS.—Here we will gather, etc.

Enter Attendant Spirit.]

          SPIRIT.

    Fair Liberty, two men from foreign shores
    Stand waiting entrance at your temple doors;
    They would the face of Freedom's mistress see;
    What shall my answer to their message be?

          LIBERTY.

    Admit them, and at once.   *[Exit Spirit.*
          Our doors are wide:
    Let the whole world flock in at every side!
    Remember Liberty, with smiling face,
    Can look on every tongue, and creed, and race!

Re-enter Spirit, with German and Irishman.]

          LIBERTY.

    Men from a foreign shore be free of speech,
    Tell us at once what blessings you would reach;
    The first: What would you—man whose ruddy face
    Shows that yours is the grand old Saxon race?

          GERMAN.

    Oh! Goddess fair! my dreams long have you filled,
    And neither king nor poverty has chilled
    The brave old German search for Liberty,
    Which to thy clime now turns instinctively.
    No goods have I. [But with my anxious hands,
    I'll clear thy teeming, broad, yet virgin lands;

Beside my Schiller place thy Washington;
Beside thy carbine, stack my needle gun.

LIBERTY.

'Tis bravely said. I know you'll keep your word,
And seal it too, if needs be, with your sword.
Your frugal race I prize. Go, choose your spot,
And in a twelvemonth, own a house and lot.
And you, the next, speak boldly as you can—
What do *you* want, good-looking Irishman?

IRISHMAN.

Be jabers! does her honor spake to me?
Come, Patrick, where's your manners? Mem, you see
A bit of land I'm wanting—not too big—
Where I can raise some praties, and dance a jig
On my own turf. No landlords, do ye mind,
For thim, and scarlet coats, I left behind.
I'll wear the blue, except, upon me soul,
Just one green sprig from this top buttonhole,
You'll not mind that. My motto's easy said:
The blue above the green, but the green above the red.

LIBERTY.

Well, take it Paddy. Go and pick the best,
On the free prairies of the great Northwest.
Oh Erin! that a sister queen might rise
To rule thee, sorrowing isle! But Paddy wipe your eyes,
Be a good Neutral. Honor every law,
And don't be over-fast to annex Canada.
My children, let these men of Europe hear,
What the three colors are to Union dear.

SEMI-CHORUS AND CHORUS.

AIR—"*Red, White and Blue.*"

Three colors there are in our banner,
 And long they have floated in pride,
From the ice of the North to the tropics,
 Fair Liberty's beacon and guide.
They were born in the heavens above us,
 Every morning revives them anew;
In the eyes, lips and cheeks of our maidens
 Ever flourish the Red, White and Blue.

CHORUS—Then hurrah for the Red, White and Blue!
 Hurrah for the Red, White and Blue!
As the glory and boast of our banner,
 Ever flourish the Red, White and Blue!

Let the men of all peoples and nations,
 From earth's farthest and loveliest isle,
Find a home 'neath our national colors—
 Come hither and bask in their smile!

Ever dear are the folds of our banner,
  For it symbols the good and the true;
We will die ere we sully or stain it—
  Ever flourish the Red, White and Blue.
CHORUS—Then hurrah, etc.

LIBERTY (*to Spirit*).
Dismiss them now—they know us as we are;
The whole world smiles beneath our Western Star.
  [*Exit Spirit, German, and Irishman.*
Enter Negro Boy.]

LIBERTY.
Why in the name of patience who are you?
Who knows where this black fellow ever grew?

NEGRO BOY.
He! he! I'm little Sambo—don't you see?
Good evening, white folks,—what do you think of me?

SOUTH CAROLINA.
Well! Is he pretty?

MASSACHUSETTS.
    No! All smutty-faced;
But honest hearts oft homely forms have graced.

SOUTH CAROLINA (*satirically*).
You're quite poetic o'er his woolly poll.

GEORGIA.
Yes, very!

ALABAMA.
  P'shaw!

VERMONT.
    No, but he has a soul.

MASSACHUSETTS.
He is not fair nor pleasant to the eye,
But has the right of happiness. Can you that truth deny?

SOUTH CAROLINA.
Oh! I don't care what your fine thoughts may be,
I *own* him: he shall *always* work for me.

MASSACHUSETTS.
Shame, sister!

SOUTH CAROLINA.
  Hold your tongue!

LIBERTY.
      Peace, children, peace;
Pray let this hot and angry quarrel cease.

SOUTH CAROLINA (*coming forward*).
Come, boy.

MASSACHUSETTS (*coming forward*).
You shall not take him for a slave,
His right to freedom the Great Father gave.
GEORGIA (*coming forward*).
If Carolina wants that little nig,
Why she may have him—so don't *you* look big.
VERMONT (*coming forward*).
I say she shan't.
SOUTH CAROLINA.
I say I will.
MASSACHUSETTS.
You won't.
GEORGIA.
You'll see.
SOUTH CAROLINA.
There'll be a pretty row, then, if I don't.

GRAND DISUNION CHORUS.

LIBERTY.
Shame! shame, my children. What will people think—
That you have had too much champagne to drink!
You that have borne the very worst of ills,
And know no discord in your several wills—
Fall out about a little darkey boy,
And all your power and all your good destroy.
Oh, shame! think better of this mad dispute,
Nor lay the blighting axe at Freedom's root.

SOUTH CAROLINA.
I wanted him to hoe my cotton field,
And I to such disgrace will never yield!

MASSACHUSETTS.
What will you do about it?

SOUTH CAROLINA.
Go away,
And have no friendship with you from this day.

LIBERTY.
That word is *treason!*

SOUTH CAROLINA.
Be it treason, then.
I'll never fellow with that pack again!

GEORGIA (*coming to her*).
Nor I!

ALABAMA (*coming to her*).
Nor I!

MISSISSIPPI (*coming to her*).
Nor I!
LOUISIANA (*coming to her*).
Nor I!
FLORIDA (*coming to her*).
Nor I!
TEXAS (*coming to her*).
And with the rest I bid you all good-bye!

LIBERTY.
Why, all of you seven must be mad, I fear!
Where are you going?

SOUTH CAROLINA.
Anywhere but *here!*

MASSACHUSETTS.
Well, let them go!

VERMONT.
Yes, let them, if they *dare!*
They'll soon find out the difference in the air!

LIBERTY.
Silence! have you no feelings left of good?
Have you forgotten all of olden blood?
Is all the glory gone from Eutaw's fight,
To those who live on Boston's storied height?
Will Carolina—*dare* she, if she will—
Forget the clustering thoughts of Bunker Hill?
Can't be that foes grow up from dearest friends,
And one sad hour a nation's destiny ends?
Forget your quarrel! there—shake hands and kiss,
And laugh next hour at what was wrong in this.

SOUTH CAROLINA.
No, never!

MASSACHUSETTS.
I don't care! and yet, I *do!*
By rights I ought to run the traitor through!

SOUTH CAROLINA.
Come on! I'd like to see you do it, Miss!
The rattle-snake is rousing—hear him hiss!
A storm is shaking the Palmetto tree.
I'd like to see you shake a spear at *me!*

VERMONT.
Don't talk of going out, or I shall strike!

GEORGIA.
We *will* go out. Now try it if you like.

New York and New Jersey intercede.]

NEW YORK.
Put down your spears. Before you tempt your fate,
Remember *I* am here—the *Empire State!*

Old Saratoga's battle-field is green,
But I remember all that soil has seen,
And not a drop of kindred blood shall flow,
But both sides number me a deadly foe!

NEW JERSEY.

My soil is scanty, and my bounds are small,
But I can count more battles than you all!
Princeton and Trenton—Monmouth—all are mine,
And I forbid you crossing peace's line.

LIBERTY.

Are you persuaded to your duty?

SOUTH CAROLINA.

No.
We've said that we go out, and out we go.

[*Cotton States secede.*

[*Re-enter Attendant Spirit in alarm.*]

SPIRIT.   [*Troubled Music.*

Oh, mistress, mistress, all our hope is lost,
Built up through all these years at heavy cost!
We thought their threat was but an idle brag,
But, mistress, they have fired upon the flag!
Against Fort Sumter hear the cannon roar,
And blood runs down the streets of Baltimore.

LIBERTY.

My children, oh my children, can it be?
You kill yourselves, alas and murder me.

SONG AND CHORUS—The first gun is fired.

The first gun is fired,
  May God protect the right,
Let the free-born sons of the North arise
  In power's avenging might;
Shall the glorious Union our fathers made,
  By ruthless hands be sundered,
And we of freedom's sacred rights
  By trait'rous foes be plundered?
Arise! Arise! Arise!
  And gird ye for the fight,
And let our watchword ever be,
  "May God protect the right."

CHORUS—Arise, etc.

END OF PART I.

["Tramp, Tramp," "The First Gun is Fired," and "The Battle Cry of Freedom," are used by permission of Root & Cady, Music Publishers, Chicago, Ill.; also, "Our Country's in Danger," by permission of H. M. Higgins, Publisher, Chicago, Ill.]

STEINWAY & SONS'
GRAND, SQUARE AND UPRIGHT
PIANO FORTES

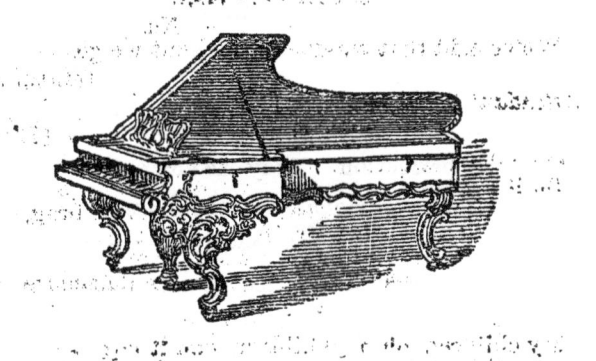

Are now considered the best in Europe, as well as in the United States, having received

THE FIRST PREMIUM

Where and whenever exhibited in competition with those of the best makers of

Boston, New York, Philadelphia and Baltimore,

As well as

LONDON, PARIS AND VIENNA.

The Jurors comprising such well-known Artists as GOTTSCHALK and WM. MASON in this country, and M. FETIS, Director of the Conservatory of Brussels, (Belgium), who was one of the Jurors of the Great International Exhibition in 1862, London, and the highest musical authority in Europe.

LETTER

FROM

THE ARTISTS OF THE ITALIAN AND GERMAN OPERA AND OTHER CELEBRATED VOCALISTS.

NEW YORK, December, 1864.

Messrs. STEINWAY & SONS:

Gentlemen,—Having used your Pianos for some time in public and in private, we desire to express our unqualified admiration in regard to their merits.

We find in them excellencies which no other pianos known to us possess to the same perfection. They are characterized by a sonority, harmonious roundness and richness of tone, combined with an astonishing prolongation of sound, most beautifully blending with and supporting the voice, to a degree that leaves nothing to be desired. Indeed, we have never met with any instruments, not even of the most celebrated manufactories of Europe, which have given us such entire satisfaction, especially as regards their unequalled qualities for accompanying the voice, and keeping in tune for so long a time, as your Pianos, and we therefore cheerfully recommend them before all others, to students of vocal music and to the public generally.

MAX MARETZEK,	F. L. QUINT,
B. MASSIMILIANI,	GIUSEPPE TAMARO,
FERD. BELLINI,	ISIDOR LEHMANN,
W. LOTTI,	H. STEINECKE,
JOS. WEINLICH,	CARL ANSCHUTZ,
MAZZOLENI,	KARL FORMES,
CARLOTTA CAROZZI ZUCCHI,	THEO. HABELMANN,
MRS. JENNIE VAN ZANDT,	FRANZ HIMMER,
CARL BERGMANN,	JOS. HERMANNS,
ELENA D'ANGRI,	BERTHA JOHANNSEN,
PEDRO DE ABELLA,	MARIE FREDERICI,
E. MILLET,	PAULINE CANISSA.

TESTIMONIAL

From the most distinguished Artists to

STEINWAY & SONS.

THE Pianofortes, Grand, Square and Upright, manufactured by Messrs. "STEINWAY & SONS," have established for themselves so world-wide a reputation, that it is hardly possible for us to add anything to their just fame.

Having thoroughly tested and tried these instruments personally for years, both in public and private, it becomes our pleasant duty to express our candid opinion regarding their unquestioned superiority over any other Piano known to us.

Among the chief points of their uniform excellence are:

Greatest possible depth, richness and volume of tone, combined with a rare brilliancy, clearness and perfect evenness throughout the entire scale, and above all, a surprising duration of sound, the pure and sympathetic quality of which never changes under the most delicate or powerful touch.

This peculiarity is found exclusively in the "STEINWAY" PIANO, and together with the matchless precision, elasticity and promptness of action always characterizing these instruments, as well as their unequaled durability under the severest trials, is truly surprising, and claims at once the admiration of every artist; we therefore consider the "STEINWAY" PIANOS in all respects by far the best instruments made in this country or Europe, use them solely and exclusively ourselves in public or private, and recommend them invariably to our friends and the public.

We have at different times expressed our opinion regarding the Pianos of various makers, but freely and unhesitatingly pronounce Messrs. "STEINWAY & SONS'" PIANOS, both Grand and Square, far superior to them all.

S. B. MILLS,
ROBERT GOLDBECK,
CARL WOLFSOHN,
A. DAVIS,
THEO. THOMAS,
MAX MARETZEK,
   Director of the Italian Opera,
CARL ANSCHUTZ,
   Director of the German Opera,
JOHN N. PATTISON,
ROBERT HELLER,
HENRY C. TIMM,
FRED. BRANDEIS,
F. L. RITTER.

CARL BERGMANN, Conductor
   at the Academy of Music and
   Philharmonic Society,
WILLIAM MASON,
ALFRED H. PEASE,
F. VON BREUNING,
THEO. SCHREINER,
E. MUZIO,
THEO. EISFELD, Conductor of
   the N. Y. and Brooklyn Phil
   Concerts.
GEO. W. MORGAN, Organist of
   Grace Church.

(See outside cover.)

PART II.

Soldier and Lady.]

SONG AND CHORUS.
Hark! my love, the Drums are Beating.

Hark, my love, the drums are beating,
  Honor bids me go,
Where the dauntless braves are meeting
  With a desperate foe.
Where Columbia's flag is streaming
  Proudly in the sky—
Oh, how vain is love's soft dreaming,
  Dry thy tearful eye.

CHORUS—When our flag victorious
  As of old shall shine,
Oh, then we'll meet again forever,
  And thou shall be mine.

Weep not, for I'll soon be coming
  Back to home and thee,
And you'll hear the millions cheering
  When our land is free;
When each wandering star returning
  Shall in glory shine,
Then with purer fondness yearning,
  I will claim thee mine.

CHORUS—When our flag victorious, etc.

Liberty.]

LIBERTY.

How strange and sorrowful all this appears,
How different from the by-gone peaceful years,
My children mine no longer, but on fire
With every maddening hate and fierce desire;
Brother 'gainst brother armed—sire against son,
My motto scorned—no longer "many in one."
How shall I lift my hand to scourge this crime?
And yet it must be done—and now it's time.
What ho, there, minister of wrath, appear
And let us plainly see the things we fear.
Ho, War, come forth.

War.]

WAR.

You call and I am here.
I hear your voice, and yet long years have passed,
My gentle mistress, since I heard it last.

LIBERTY.

Yes, that was nearly twenty years ago,
When first I sent you on to Mexico.
That was a foreign struggle—now, alas,
Things none believed have sadly come to pass.
It is against *ourselves* that we must fight;
And yet it must be—God defend the right.
Sound me that horn that's hanging at your side,
To send the warlike summons far and wide.
From sea to mountain, and the plains beyond,
Call all my children—see if they respond.

SONG AND CHORUS—Our Country's in Danger.

Come with your sabres and come with your guns,
Our country's in danger and calls for her sons;
Stay not for the harvest, turn back from the plow;
Our country's in danger and calls for you now.

WAR.

Hark! scarce a moment has conveyed the sound,
And yet their coming thunder shakes the ground.

LIBERTY.

They hear—they answer—It is true indeed.
They do not all desert me in my need!

Enter Loyal States, and with them a body of soldiers.]
Enter Truth and Justice, and take places by Liberty.]

CHORUS—We're coming, we are coming,
We hear the loud cry;
We'll rescue our country,
We'll save her or die.

Oh! let us rekindle the patriot fires,
That glowed in the hearts of our brave old sires!
Our watchword is "Freedom," and so we will fight,
For God and our country, the *truth* and the right.

CHORUS—We're coming, etc.

LIBERTY.

Welcome, my children, with your loyal power;
Though sad I am to see this trying hour.
I had not called, though desolation's hand
Had been outstretched above my cherished land,—
But that against this flag of stripes and stars
Secession curses and disunion wars.

TRUTH.

Shame on the hand first fired upon the flag.
That hand drop down a helpless, loathsome rag.

JUSTICE.

Gibbets for traitors who have done the wrong;
And all deceived learn better things ere long!

LIBERTY.
Do you still love the flag?

ALL.
(Hurrah!)

LIBERTY.
Then raise
A song to greet it as in other days.

THE BATTLE-CRY OF FREEDOM.—Rallying Song.

Yes, we'll rally round the flag, boys, we'll rally once again,
  Shouting the battle-cry of Freedom;
We will rally from the hill-side, we'll rally from the plain,
  Shouting the battle-cry of Freedom.

CHORUS—The Union forever, hurrah, boys, hurrah!
  Down with the tyrant, up with the star,
While we rally round the flag, boys, rally once again,
  Shouting the battle-cry of Freedom.

We are springing to the call, from the East and from the West,
  Shouting the battle-cry of Freedom,
And we'll hurl the rebel crew from the land we love the best,
  Shouting the battle-cry of Freedom.

CHORUS—The Union forever, hurrah, boys, hurrah!

NEW YORK.
Say, did you doubt us, mistress? Did you fear
That when you called, we would not all appear?

LIBERTY.
No! I was sure to see you, every State;
I only feared you would arrive *too late.*
Southern rebellion never had been shown
Had it expected to be left alone.
The flag of treason ne'er had been displayed,
But that it hoped to gather *Northern aid!*
The North united, we can conquer all;
But woe to us if once to words *we* fall.

MASSACHUSETTS.
'Tis deeds we want, not words—for words are weak,
So briefly let us all our fealty speak;
And I, as eldest of the Eastern band,
Will say what means the brave old Yankee land:
We gave you Warren, Stark, and brave old Put,
When on us first Oppression's fingers shut.

Both Bunker Hill and Lexington were ours,
When on you Europe poured her hireling powers.
We conquered in the name of Freedom then,
And all we ask, is to be tried again.

NEW-YORK.

I, too, will speak, as all the country waits,
For all my sisters of the Middle States.
Upon *our* soil, by blood of Freemen bought,
The battles of our liberty were fought.
Trenton was Jersey's, Saratoga mine,
And Pennsylvania's bloody Brandywine;
And little Delaware had given a tomb
To many a Hessian, if she had but room.
But aid us while we tell you in a song,
How all the loyal States come marching along.

SEMI-CHORUS AND CHORUS.

AIR—"*Tramp, Tramp.*"

Oh! we heed thy trumpet call,
We are coming, one and all;
 Each patriot heart has sworn thy banner bright
Shall float from sea to sea,
And its folds be shaken free
 From the traitor hand that would its glory blight.

CHORUS—Tramp! tramp! tramp! the States are marching,
 Hark! they gather near and far,
  With the music's thrilling clash
  And the musket's vivid flash,
 And a flag o'er head that blazons every star.

Though the victory be delayed
We will never be dismayed;
 Through sunshine and through storm we'll press the fray,
While a drop runs in our veins
Or a jewel yet remains,
 We'll proudly yield them up to win the day.

CHORUS—Tramp! tramp! etc.

OHIO.

And I must speak, I think, for all the rest—
My fair young sisters of the giant West.
No foot of slave has trampled soil of mine,
But freedom gushes, like my generous wine.
We love the flag; suppose that music's breath
Should sound our motto—"Liberty or Death."

SONG.—The Watchword—"Liberty or Death."

Liberty, Liberty, Liberty, or Death!
The land awakens at the shout,

Fling on your flags the watchword out!
Give to the battle bugle breath,
And welcome Liberty or Death!
    Liberty or Death!
With that watchword waving o'er us,
Where's the foe can stand before us?
    Liberty, or Death, etc.

NEW JERSEY.

Ha! ha! what's this meets our vision now?
Some people look as if they'd seen a row.

Enter Seceded States, in ragged costume, bearing the Rebel Flag.]

MASSACHUSETTS.

What is't you want, you quick-returning seven?
Come back already then, to be forgiven?

SOUTH CAROLINA.

We only come to go away again
And take the Border Sisters in our train,
North Carolina, Maryland, Tennessee,
Virginia, Kentucky and Missouri.
Arkansas and Delaware, no more delay,
But with your Southern leaders come away.
Hark to the voice that rouses all your pride,
And call you loudly to Secession's side.

CHORUS—Seceded to Border States.

AIR—"Come to the Bower."

Will you join with Carolina and her Sisters of the South?
Will you hearken to the warning voice from every Southern mouth?
On your cherished institution has the mark of wrong been put,
And soon you will be trampled by the Northern tyrant's foot.
    ‖:Will you, will you, will you, will you—join with the South?:‖

On your rights the scoffers tread, as the British did of old:
Has the blood within your veins grown all passionless and cold?
Let them feel that Southern pulses have their heat from Southern suns,
And that Liberty's red tide with its olden current runs!
    Will you, will you, etc.

TENNESSEE.

I should not go, for Andrew Jackson's sake—
The man whose Union love no wrong could break.
But some of you have tried to use me ill,
And so, to spite you—yes, I think I will.
    [Goes over to the Seceded States.

KENTUCKY.

I think you miss it, sister. If you doubt,
Ask Parson Brownlow, now that he is out,
I cannot leave the Union for a day,
Without a curse from the dead Henry Clay.

DELAWARE.

I am the least, they say, of all my kind;
Yet I'm too big and old to be so blind.
If any body hears that *I* shall go,
I hope they'll take the pains to let me know.

NORTH CAROLINA.

I always hated South Carolina. Pshaw!
I always hated worse your Northern law.
Away I go, with all my fat pitch-pine,
What will they do for tar and turpentine?
　　　　　　　　　　　[*Goes over to the Seceded States.*

DELAWARE.

At tar and turpentine we well may smile
For all along *our* lines *we're* striking *ile.*

MARYLAND.

My monuments are all for patriot sons;
I have no room for raising traitor ones.
You cannot tempt me. None like me deplore
That sad first blood they shed in Baltimore.

MISSOURI.

I am a member of the giant West,
And know the Union bond will bind me best.
I like the nigger pretty well, no doubt,
But think that I can get along without.

ARKANSAS.

I had outgrown you all these ten years back,
But don't try tricks on bluff old Rackensack.
I've no idea what it is all about,
But South Carolina calls,—and I go out.
　　　　　　　　　　　[*Goes over to the Seceded States.*

VIRGINIA.

I had a motive stronger than you all,
To keep me ever at the Union's call.
Fortune to me the highest honor gave—
I furnished Washington both birth and grave.
My fields, with Northern capital enriched,
My sandy wastes improved, my marshes ditched,
I might be, did I slight this tempting call,
In twenty years the wealthiest of you all.
And yet I'm going in my State Rights' pride
To do a little bit of suicide.
　　　　　　　　　　　[*Goes over to the Seceded States.*

NEW YORK.

Oh, stop, Virginia; do not go, I pray.

NEW JERSEY.

Pause. pause, Virginia—drive this thought away,
Don't go, at least, until we try once more
To stir the memories of your patriot shore.

CHORUS—Loyal to Seceded States.
AIR—"*Bell Brandon.*"

There's a home down in old Virginia,
  By the fair Potomac's woody shore,
Where the hearts of the nation are turning,
  And the world shall be looking evermore.
In that home lived the Father of his country;
  There the home of his children yet must be!
Oh that grave must belong to his people—
  Mount Vernon's the Mecca of the Free.

There were squalor and ruin around it,
  In the hand of the miserly it lay;
But the hands of America's daughters
  Have swept the polluting stain away.
Southern matrons have found northern mothers
  Leagued as one from the mountains to the sea;
And his grave must belong to the Union!
  Mount Vernon's the Mecca of the Free!

SOUTH CAROLINA.

There's four, at least, have answered to our call,
A little longer we shall have them *all.*

VERMONT.

Will you? I should like to see you do it, then!
You win no battles, and you've got no *men!*

SOUTH CAROLINA (*tauntingly*).

Oh, don't we? Very nice that game will be!
Where's *Stonewall Jackson?* What d'ye think of *Lee?*
Seen *Morgan* lately? What last Yankee load
Went into Richmond by the *Mosby* road?
You have more men and rations, I confess,
And rather beat us marching, too, I guess.
For it took you three good days to reach Bull Run,
While to return you needed only one.

OHIO.

Oh pray proceed: your taunts we wont repress,
For out of failure we will pluck success.
To win we've wholly pledged our treasures vast,
And he laughs best, remember, who laughs last.
We've dashed your monarch Cotton from his throne,
And still our granaries with plenty groan.
Our gallant boys have plumpest haversacks,
And pockets lined with good-as-gold greenbacks.
Disparage Lee we will not, may be can't;
Only we'll rout him with one U. S. Grant,
Who late at Vicksburg raised the conqueror's shout,
And now on this line cooly fights it out.

SOUTH CAROLINA.
Don't be too sure of that!
OHIO.
Of course not. No!
But will you show me *where he once let go?*
SOUTH CAROLINA.
Humph, well—
NEW YORK.
There, you can't do it, so don't try!
We'll *dampen* you, next time, if that is dry;
Give you a taste of FARRAGUT the brave,
The modern Viking of the Western wave,
The man who took *New Orleans,* just in play,
And show'd his *earnest* down in *Mobile Bay!*
Then we have PORTER—

GEORGIA.
Oh, do stop your boast.

MASSACHUSETTS.
Can't till we name a *few* more of the host.
You don't like sailors? Well then take a man
Who sweeps a *valley* out like SHERIDAN;
Or one who knocks apart the rebel arch
By history's longest and most daring march,—
He who can dwarf Napoleon's Russian fame,
And over Xenophon's write SHERMAN'S name!

LIBERTY.
There, that will do. Pray let the record be
What you can do to foes beyond the sea.
Who knows but while you raise the noisy din,
Some foreign foe, invited, may step in
And dim the sod upon your father's graves,
By making you, and all who tread them, slaves.

SOUTH CAROLINA.
Well, let it be so.
VIRGINIA.
Hem. I don't quite know
How that would do—to brook a foreign foe.
NEW YORK.
I know then—Europe ne'er gains fame or spoil
By planting hostile foot on Western soil.

SONG AND CHORUS—The Realm of the West.

Have you heard of the beautiful Realm of the West,
  Encircled by oceans, and kissed by the sun?
Have you heard of the nations that thrive on her breast,
  Bright heirs of her grandeur, the "Many in one?"

CHORUS—Kings cannot govern this land of our choice,
  Liberty loves us, and peace is our guest;
  Shout for the Union with heart and with voice
  God is our king in this Realm of the West.

Have you seen our brave men? they are noble and true;
The fame has gone forth of the deeds they have done,
For when right led the van, to the conflict they flew,
  And victory greeted the "Many in one!"

CHORUS—Kings cannot govern, etc.

SOUTH CAROLINA.

That song don't suit me now.

MASSACHUSETTS.

  I dare say not.
It don't suit a dark secession plot.

NEW JERSEY.

Say, Carolina, softly in your ear—
Isn't it colder, rather, there than here?
Isn't your *glory* quite an empty sound,
With bacon worth ten dollars to the pound.
And whisky so *unreasonably* high,
There's nothing left but villainous old rye.

SOUTH CAROLINA.

Well that does pinch, I own it. Rum and salt
Are things we hate to lose by any fault.
Things had no need to be in such a shape:
'Twas Floyd and Davis got us in the scrape;
And—

NEW YORK.

  You'll come out again, of course, at once?

SOUTH CAROLINA.

No; if I do, then set me down a dunce—
People may hold a right and hold it strong,
Nothing for me like sticking to a *wrong*.

Enter Foreign Intervention.]

LIBERTY.

Well, who are *you!*

INTERVENTION.

  One who but waits a chance—
The meddling soul of England and of France,
They call me Foreign Intervention; you
Have just been giving me some work to do.

MASSACHUSETTS.

Get out.

NEW YORK.

  Yes, and the sooner that you go,
Why that will be the quicker, don't you know?

SOUTH CAROLINA.
No, stay. Now things assume a better shape,
Who knows but you can clear us from the scrape?

LIBERTY.
Old Europe's threatening son,
That may be something easier said than done.

INTERVENTION.
You cannot stop me if I choose to come:
We've Alabamas by the score, at home.

LIBERTY.
And we can raise, whene'er the prize grows large,
Just here and there another *Kearsarge*,
To give your *Semmes* another raking blast
And change our WIN-SLOW's name to be WIN-FAST!

INTERVENTION.
Then I'm not welcome?

SOUTH CAROLINA.
Yes.

NEW YORK.
I tell you, no.

INTERVENTION.
The last one's biggest, and I think I'll go.
[*Starts off, then pauses.*
Adieu, Queen of the *Dis*-United States,
Who to King George proved such absurd ingrates.
I'll go back home, encourage neutral trade,
Hob-nob with Semmes, and sneer at your blockade.
A little cotton still perhaps I'll run
By Stono Inlet or by Wilmington—
And pay for it in English shot and ball.
To kill—its no affair of mine—that's all.

LIBERTY.
I scorn your threats! you think my hands are tied,
But were you 'gainst me openly allied,
I'd drive your armies from my sacred shore
And crush your navies as I've done before.
You have no appetite for fighting me
Unless you're screened behind neutrality.
Take heed lest all your powder, ball and shot
Fly back at you from Yankee cannon hot.
I know you well; you menace or you fawn,
As nations prosper. Sordid wretch, *be gone.*

[*Exit Foreign Intervention and Seceded States.*
Enter Western Virginia and Nevada.]

SONG OF WELCOME.

Air—"*Union and Liberty.*"

Hail to the States as they enter the Union
Far from the wilds of the limitless West.
Who shall dissolve the dear bond that unites us.
||:Honor has sealed it, and Freedom has blessed.:||

Chorus—Up with our banner bright, sprinkled with starry light,
Spread its fair emblems from mountain to shore;
While through the sounding sky, loud rings the nation's cry,
:||Union and Liberty! one evermore!||:

Enter Negro Boy.]

NEGRO BOY.

Well, white folks, here I is agin, you see.
I golly dis nigger now is clar made free.
I'm no great scholar, but I've larned to spell,
And dis is my first lesson! yah! yah! Well,
'Twas Massa Lincum writ dis to de nation,
And called it de Emancipation Proclamation.
He says he'll not hab niggers hoein' corn
To feed de worstest traitors eber born;
And if dey don't repent, dere slaves will be
Dere slaves no longer, but foreber free.
And from dat day we've lub'd de Yankee boys,
To serb and shield dem was our greatest joys.
We baked dem corn bread till de meal was out,
Helped dem from prison, hid de wounded scout;
Cooked for de Captain and the sojers' mess,
And done a little fightin', too, I guess.
I'm lookin' now for somfin dat will pay,
Somfin 'spectable—terms—two dollars a day.
Who wants me? what's dat? Well, if I can't trade
I'll 'list as corporal in de black brigade.

[*Exit Negro Boy.*

LIBERTY.

My heart sinks low with fear.
I think I know what dreadful forms appear.

Re-enter Rebel States, pursued by War, Famine and Pestilence.]

WAR.

My work is doing. Desolation reigns
In crowded cities and on fertile plains;
The nation's wealth is fading like a mist,
War rules, and nothing can the fate resist.

FAMINE.

The country has not known *me* since its birth,
Famine—the deadliest foe of man on earth.

Your quarrels call me—all must feel my pains,
If the black fiend, Disunion, here remains.

PESTILENCE.

My name is Pestilence. I come from far,
In the same track that brings you Want and War.
My fevered breath a deadly plague is found,
Where slaughtered men unburied strew the ground;
Persist in war, and thicker grows the gloom
Until I sweep you to one common tomb.

LIBERTY.

Great heavens. Their words are true. Each horrid shape
Tells but the truth. And is there no escape?

TRUTH.

But one. Restore again the Union bond,
And pray to Heaven that rules all things beyond.

LIBERTY.

Her words are true. Lost children, doomed of Heaven,
Kneel lowly down—you yet may be forgiven.

PRAYER—CHORUS.

AIR—"*Old Hundred.*"

Father in Heaven! in peace look down;
Withdraw once more thine angry frown;
Forgive the sins our lives that stain,
And make us happy once again.

WAR.

Your prayer is vain—your line is broken still;
Pestilence, War and Famine have their will.

[*Enter a Messenger in haste.*]

LIBERTY.

Shout all! The long-tried work at last is done!
Lee has surrendered, and the fight is won!
The stronghold of rebellion doffs the rag
Of treason, and hauls up the good old flag.

ALL (*enthusiastically.*)

Hurrah!

[*Exit Rebel States.*

OHIO.

Now shout once more, before you can't,
For those who did it—Sherman, Sheridan, Grant,
And all the brave men, field, staff, rank and file,
Who fought and won 'neath heaven's approving smile!

Hurrah!
                ALL.
                [*Exit War, Famine and Pestilence, muttering.*
Re-enter Rebel States and resume their places in the Union.]
           NEW YORK.
See what disunion does. Before 'tis o'er,
It gives up all the lost, and adds two more.
Enter Army of the Potomac and Sherman's Bummers.]

SONG AND CHORUS.

AIR—"*When Johnny Comes Marching Home.*"

'Tis Johnny comes marching home again, hurrah, hurrah,
We'll give him a hearty welcome now, hurrah, hurrah;
The men will cheer, the boys will shout,
The ladies they will all turn out,
And we'll all feel gay, now Johnny comes marching home.

Let love and friendship on this day, hurrah, hurrah,
Their choicest treasures now display, hurrah, hurrah;
And let each one perform some part,
To fill with joy the warrior's heart,
And we'll, etc.

           LIBERTY.

All hail, bronzed heroes! Hail my glorious braves,
Hail to the battle-flag that o'er ye waves!
Thy valor plants it where no others fly
And blazons it with matchless victory.
Thy missing comrades for it fought and fell,
The nation grieves but loves them—oh! how well.
For you and them a wond'ring world sings fame,
And freemen all greet you with wild acclaim.
All's saved, my children; and by Heaven's good will,
Still other stars our nation's sky shall fill.
Our darkest hour was just before the day;
Our fear, the moment trouble, fled away.
God guards the nations—He will not forsake
This land, commissioned Slavery's chain to break
All praise to Him; let the chorus rise,
Loudly and proudly to the favoring skies,
When Union triumphs and Disunion dies.

STAND BY THE BANNER OF COLUMBIA.

Fairest land beneath the sun, the cradle of the brave,
Given to thy keeping is sweet Liberty to save!
O'er no haughty despot shall thy starry banner wave
    'Tis the flag of the brave and the free!

CHORUS—‖:Hurrah for the colors of Columbia!:‖
Stand by the banner of Columbia!
'Tis the flag of the brave and the free.

O'er our Country, o'er our Flag, and o'er our nation's fame,
Watching with a pure delight sweet Freedom's living flame,
Dwells our sainted *Washington!* We glorify his name.
With the flag of the brave and the free.
CHORUS—Hurrah, etc.

LIBERTY.

Then, now at once, from shore to shore,
My sister, Peace, may hold her sway once more.

Enter Second Messenger.]

SECOND MESSENGER.

Hold! do not speak one word of joy or peace!
Let all the new-born hopes of freemen cease!
Our PRESIDENT, beloved of all the land,
Lies foully murdered by a traitor's hand.

MASSACHUSETTS.

Oh, horrible!

ALL.

Most horrible!

ILLINOIS.

Alas! alas! this is truly the worst
Of all the deeds that history's page has cursed!
To slay the great and brave, just when he stood
Proclaiming mercy for the whole land's good!
What was his fault? A heart with love o'errun
"With charity for all—with malice toward none;"
These were thy words, my greatest, best-loved son.
Give me my dead—the precious dust return
To me—to me. In honor's costliest urn
I'll place it tenderly and guard it well,
And water it with tears.

MASSACHUSETTS.

Toll, toll the bell!
Drape every house in mourning, far and near!
Let a whole people weep above his bier!
Let the world shudder, that the Borgia's crime
Has come to blast us in our Western clime!

MARYLAND.

Oh, horror! that my soul has given birth
To such a monster. All that I am worth
I'd give, could I recall into that lifeless form
The God-like soul—life's current rich and warm.
Let earth to such a murderer give no spot
Of rest, until he starve, and die, and rot!

NEW YORK.
Aye! let the hand of might be swift and strong
To slay the author of so foul a wrong!
Enter Third Messenger.]
THIRD MESSENGER.
Your wish is granted, almost in the breath!
The assassin met a quick and bloody death!
NEW YORK.
Insensate wretch! To think this noble land
Could be destroyed by an assassin hand:
Our march is onward. Presidents may fall,
Yet Liberty survives to bless us all.
Though leaders perish, and turn traitors, too,
The hand of God will safely lead us through.
No single arm shall wreck the ship of state;
The *people* rule; *their* ballots thunder fate.
LIBERTY.
And see the spectacle we set the world,
Who 'gainst our might so many lips have curled.
Men die, but the Republic's living still,
And has a thousand years, in God's good will.
Welcome, thrice welcome, to this glorious day,
For treason cannot blight nor murder slay
The fair young Freedom, who this many a year
Has truly blest this Western hemisphere.
Our nation's golden sunrise seems to break
And weds in glory river, cliff and lake.
The springs that rise and travel to the sea
Shall touch no shore that knows not Liberty.
Errors shall be forgotten, discord cease,
For Union triumphs! welcome, dove-eyed Peace.
Enter Peace.]
PEACE.
"God of Peace! whose spirit fills
All the echoes of our hills,
All the murmurs of our rills,
Now the storm is o'er;
Oh! let freemen be our sons,
And let future Washingtons
Rise to lead their valiant ones,
'Till there's war no more."

SONG AND CHORUS.

AIR—"*Star-Spangled Banner.*"
Oh thus be it ever, when freemen shall stand
Between the loved homes and the war's desolation;
Blest with victory and peace, may the Heaven-rescued land
Praise the power that has made and preserved us a nation.
CHORUS—Then conquer we must, when our cause it is just,
And this be our motto—"In God is our trust!"
FULL CHORUS—And the star-spangled banner in triumph shall wave
O'er the land of the free and the home of the brave.

[*See Grand Final Tableau next page.*]

GRAND FINAL TABLEAU OF PEACE.

CENTER PIECE.
1.—Goddess of Liberty, crowning a maimed soldier.
2.—Attendant Spirit kneeling.
3.—War, Famine and Pestilence overcome and prostrate.

RIGHT OF CENTER.
1.—Peace, hoped for, and at last attained.
2.—Ceres, Goddess of the Harvest, bearing a sheaf of wheat.
3.—Soldier and lady, the absent returned, and group listening to the hero's story.
4.—Illinois confronted by messengers who bring the sad tidings of Lincoln's martyrdom, and offer consolation.
5.—Child with musket, emblematic of Peace regained.

LEFT OF CENTER.
1.—Massachusetts and South Carolina, out of the deadly breach, now clasp hands over the negro freed from bondage.
2.—Group listening to a soldier, just returned from the war, who tells of a brother soldier's heroism and his death.

MISCELLANEOUS DISPOSITION.
1.—On the extreme right and left of the stage are the soldiers of the Army of the Potomac, Sherman's Bummers, and other "boys in blue," who have stacked arms and rejoice that the conflict is o'er.
2.—In the rear is a semi-circle of States, arranged North and South alternately, with spears crossed once again in the bonds of peace and fraternal Union.
3.—Still further in the rear are trains and soldiers, viewing the scene as one of bright promise to the whole nation.
4.—Emigrants—German and Irishman.
5.—Foreign Intervention frantic with joy—of course!!

To give effect to the Tableau, red lights are produced, and the audience are requested to remain in their seats until the full scene is brought out. The press, wherever the Tableau has been presented, have pronounced it the **FINEST ALLEGORICAL REPRESENTATION** ever arranged upon the Stage for the public eye.

The spectator will see its beauties more forcibly by studying the historical points aimed to be presented, while, at the same time, noting the scenic arrangements.

12) 350
    30

THE SPLENDID OVERSTRUNG
Grand Piano Fortes

USED AT THESE ENTERTAINMENTS,

Are from the extensive and world-renowned establishment of

STEINWAY & SONS,
NEW YORK,

Which will be no small Feature in the Entertainment.

These Pianos have delighted thousands in this country and Europe, and now stand without a rival in the World, as will appear by the following:

GREAT TRIUMPH.

STEINWAY & SONS, New York, have been awarded a FIRST PRIZE MEDAL at the Grand International Exhibition, London, "For powerful, clear, brilliant and sympathetic tone, with excellent workmanship, as shown in GRAND AND SQUARE PIANOS."

There were two hundred and sixty-nine Pianos from all parts of the world, entered for competition; and the special correspondent of the *Times* says:

"Messrs. Steinway's indorsement by the jurors is emphatic and stronger and more to the point than that of any European maker."

Extracts from the London "Court Gazette."

W. B. PAPE, the young American Pianist, played with great success before the Queen and Guests at the grand Reception after the Wedding of the Prince of Wales at Windsor Castle, upon a Grand Piano made by STEINWAY & SONS, New York. The Piano used at the Castle is the one which took the First Medal at the World's Fair, London, 1862.

WAREROOMS,
Nos. 71 and 73 East Fourteenth Street,

Between Union Square and the Academy of Music.

CPSIA information can be obtained
at www.ICGtesting.com
Printed in the USA
LVHW011357111218
600055LV00004B/460/P